GW00381426

BURSTING THE CLOUDS

BY THE SAME AUTHOR

The Imbolc Bride

BURSTING THE CLOUDS

John Sewell

CAPE POETRY

First published 1998

1 3 5 7 9 10 8 6 4 2

First published in the United Kingdom in 1998
by Jonathan Cape,
Random House, 20 Vauxhall Bridge Road, London SW1V 2SA

Random House Australia (Pty) Limited
20 Alfred Street, Milsons Point, Sydney,
New South Wales 2061, Australia

Random House New Zealand Limited
18 Poland Road, Glenfield,
Auckland 10, New Zealand

Random House South Africa (Pty) Limited
Endulini, 5A Jubilee Road, Parktown 2193, South Africa

Random House UK Limited Reg. No. 954009

A CIP catalogue record for this book
is available from the British Library

Papers used by Random House UK Limited are natural,
recyclable products made from wood grown in sustainable forests.
The manufacturing processes conform to the environmental
regulations of the country of origin.

ISBN 0-224-05118-0

Typeset by Palimpsest Book Production Limited,
Polmont, Stirlingshire
Printed and bound in Great Britain by
Creative Print and Design (Wales), Ebbw Vale

For Liz & Dave

Off a side road, draw in behind
the parked Sierra, dusky blue.

Two blackbirds are chasing up and
down the mounds of chippings.

One trails a loose tail feather
in her brown tail.

Effing and blinding no doubt,
they sit up suddenly, the two

in front, sort themselves out,
clip seat belts, slip away.

CONTENTS

IV SCENES FROM THE CUTTING-ROOM FLOOR

ACKNOWLEDGEMENTS

Some of the poems have appeared in the following:

Ambit; *Arvon Poetry Competition Anthology '87*; *'Draft #2' – Anthology of Poetry at the Albert, Huddersfield '95*; *'Final Draft' – Anthology of Poetry at the Albert, Huddersfield '96*; *Giant Steps*; *Iron*; *Lancaster Literature Festival Poetry Competition Anthology '96*; *Observer; Poetry Book Society Anthologies '87, '91*; *Poetry Durham*; *Poetry Society National Poetry Competition Anthology '92*; *Poetry Wales*; *'Sex in the 90s' – Anthology of New Writing in Sheffield '94*; *Sheffield Thursday*; *Stand*; *Staple*; *Verse*; *Wide Skirt*

'Scenes from the Cutting Room Floor' was, in an earlier form, a finalist in the Arvon International Poetry Competition, 1987.
'The Word' was a prizewinner in the National Poetry Competition, 1992.
'The Amazing Thing' won first prize in the Yorkshire Open Poetry Competition, 1993.
'Rhea's Days by Black Waterfall' won the Sheffield Thursday Prize, 1994.

The author is grateful for a Fellowship at Hawthornden Castle where many of these poems were written or completed.

I

THE WORD

THE WORD

I'm passing the room as she's bending over, folding up
the travelling table she bought that day,
and for a moment there's a softening I haven't felt
in years, that used to be there all the time,
never dreaming it could be any other way.

Later, while the News is on, I tell her how it felt
watching her fold the table to an oblong,
into a long red case. I touch her arm
briefly, as I say this. *It's just what I wanted,*
she says, *it's too cramped to eat inside the van.*

The photo on the box has a couple chatting and drinking
at the table on a summer afternoon.
Back then, I'm thinking to myself, even the collar of her coat
could make me cry. Next day I carry the table out, watch her
load and stow everything away, strap the kids in and drive.

The quiet's always strange at first, I'm upstairs half asleep
when a word comes to mind, and I'm thinking yes
that sums up the whole situation. I'm thinking I must
remember that word. I try angling for it all next day
but can't, for the life of me, think now what it is.

THE MISTAKE

I knew there was something as soon as she got back.
You're so thin, she said, as I got into the bath.
It was then she told me about Malcolm.
How they'd slept together the whole two weeks, that she
    loved him
but wasn't sure how much she loved him. Though the main
    thing was,

she still loved me, and gave me a hug to prove it.
Inviting him for the weekend seemed the best thing to do.
He was OK. We went for wine together while Jo
cooked a meal. He was lots of things I wasn't, I could see that.
Two husbands might not be such a bad idea, I was thinking.

In bed that first night, it seemed right that we both
went through to Malcolm's room. Better that,
than leaving someone out. Malcolm looked surprised
as Jo climbed in the middle. But no one said or did anything.
We just lay there on our backs, a ménage à trois in alabaster,

wondering what the hell should happen next.
That was fifteen years ago this week.
What happened next was me with Sue, then Jo
with Steve, then me with Jane, then Jo with Steve (again),
etc., etc. Malcolm, as it turned out,

was nowhere. Which suited me.
I made the mistake one day of asking Jo how it felt
with him. Fellatio, for instance.
Oh that was good, she said (making the mistake
of an honest answer). *His penis, it was such a lovely shape.*

THE AMAZING THING

Though we'd never spoken, except once in the corridors,
we started dancing, drunk enough in our paper hats
to smooch the fast ones without embarrassment. Our bodies
took us by surprise. Mid-afternoon, when we wandered back
to the office, her arm in mine all the way, I was thinking

wouldn't it be just like it, for Jo to drive past now. So I knew
when a red Peugeot appeared, the way it would go.
She was almost past when she saw me. I saw the wave, the
    mouth say
There's Daddy to Freya in the back, then her look
take in who was draped across my shoulder, and talking at that
    moment

about nothing in particular, almost to herself,
too absorbed to notice how I turned to watch the car go past
with Freya in the back craning round to face me as it vanished.
What was so amazing, Jo said later, was to see this happen,
but feel nothing, absolutely nothing. Not a thing.

THE RESPONSE

Evening, flawless.
Moon, emergent, with a single, pendant planet.
Tractor, still circling the meadow like a razor
    working to a centre that means home.
Someone, walking up the lane in front.
Window, wide open at first floor.
Woman, elbows on the sill, leaning out.
Man, behind her, hitching up her skirt.
Woman, steadying herself on the frame as he enters.
Neighbour, below now in the lane, waves.
– *Hi*, says the woman, leaning out further,
    Isn't it wonderful!
– *Wonderful.*
    – *Wonderful.* Comes the double response.

THE COLLISION

– *A car's just banged your car.*
It was Karen from three doors up. Jo asks her:
– *You mean the Peugeot, parked near the bend?*

– *You didn't park it there?* I say, *That was stupid.*
A pause. Then: – *Go on. Blame me. It's my fault.*
Every-time. I'm sick of it.

– *You sour screwed-up bitch,* I tell her. Which was
even more stupid. Freya is coming down the stairs,
opening the door as the first blow lands.

When I examine it later, all there is is a long
blue smear on the grey bumper, but nothing's
bent or sheered. This time.

Among some photos she collects that week
is one of her beside the ocean. Smiling.
It's like staring back into history.

Where was that? I ask. She knows the next thing
I'll say now is Sorry. Sorry.
At Whistling Sands, she says. *We must go sometime.*

All of us, she adds. At least I think
that's what she says. She's walking off
as she says it, talking to the wall.

THE APPRENTICESHIP

When we'd finally finished, Jo and I (*'finished'!*) yet again
the shouting, intimidations and abuse, and were somehow
(by what thread of sanity) back to our opposing corners,
I couldn't (could I) leave it at that, but had to burst in on
    Rowan,
his hands pressed to his ears, the way I pressed my own ears hard
when I was twelve and things like this went on downstairs,
pressing hard then easing off – Had it stopped yet? Had they
    finished?
more often than not, reclamping them again, harder so the
    thunder in my head
could muffle me under –
                    despite which, not content with how
    things stood,
going way beyond my parent's worst excesses, regardless
of his frightened, tearful look – I laid in on him for causing all
    this grief:
Look what you've done, I said, *Don't you learn anything.*

THE WISH

That boy doesn't have a bottom,
why doesn't he have a bottom?
My six-year-old is watching
breakfast pictures of the latest famine.
I tell him half the world is hungry,
that a boy like that would be glad
of the crusts on our plates each morning.
I'm going there, he says, *when I'm older*
with some food, so the boy can get his bottom back.

I moved out that same day,
for the second time in as many months,
to a holiday place just up the road.
Being apart seems the only way
Jo and I can stay friends.
It's a small place, in a row of four.
The walls are thin. Each evening
I hear the same child crying,
not through hunger I should think,
but tiredness or lack of love.

I tell my son about the move
as we're driving back from swimming.
It's dark outside, and cold.
It's just for a while, I tell him,
to give mum and me some space.
I think he doesn't hear, then he says,
the new house, he'd like us all
to have a holiday there.

THE SPLIT

Never had we been so happy.
Jo and I agreed, with much hugging
and kissing, to split up.

I phoned Australia, told Jane
it was her and I from now on.
Her and I. It sounded good.

I was two hours early. Her flight,
two hours late. When she finally appeared,
with her backpack, her hold-all, her twin-pack

of booze, and we rushed together –
it was not what I expected, not
how I'd imagined it to be –

that first moment of a new life.
And something in her, said the same thing back.
As we kissed and hugged, her first words were:

The bastards charged me duty on the gin.
And I've such a stinking cold. I'm sorry . . .

I never did like her, said Jo, six months
later, *I'm glad you two have split.*

Listen, are you free tonight?
There's a party on at Ann's. I've tried and tried
but can I get a babysitter?

She must have seen the let-down
in my face. I got a hug
as she was leaving. But not a kiss.

THE GAP

Out the bath and through to the fire,
she's towelling herself dry as I enter.
Her back's towards me. When she turns to speak
she holds the towel close against her.

I ask her things of no importance,
make as if the TV is of interest.
She goes on drying the same dry spot,
her nape, her upper arm, her neck.

Only when I leave the room
will she turn her back towards the fire
and let the towel fall at her feet.
Which is why I only partly close the door.

To leave a hinge-sized gap along the frame.
And why I'm out here on the landing,
bending forwards. And why nothing
(or no one) can tear me away.

II

RHEA'S DAYS BY BLACK WATERFALL

THE LAKE # 1

And all the way back down
all the way back to the cottage
we kept turning to look at the mountain

and at dusk when the mountain
filled the whole lake east to west
so the lake was the colour of the mountain

we sculled on its reflection
looking down into the depths of the mountain
the lake was a jar we spat into

to mix something of ourselves with the mountain
till we and the lake, and the lake and the mountain
could not be distinguished one from the other

looking inwards was the same
as looking outwards in that light
we ourselves were the mountain

only the sky stayed witholding and separate
then it too began to grain
and sink into the mountain

when the stars came out
everything was indivisible.

BLACK WATERFALL

I

As if courting it –
each day for three days
walking there through frosted woods.

We'd lean, weight forward
where it lunges over –
three spreading tails of water

the spray-mist glazed
on rocks, a jutting branch
englassed, each turf spike

a clear feather of ice.
Only its sound
between us.

Everything was waterfall,
no matter how furious
or slow, movement

was immaterial.
A minute went by,
then another.

From where we stood
the sky had new light –
intelligible fire.

II

Today it's a whisper,
little more than a rivulet
ladled over the lip,

mossing down in pleats and threads,
scinted on ledges.
It's a delicate matter

shifting foot to foot,
a drenched rainbow
pours onto the stone.

I'm there, irresistibly
gazing through the curtain,
drawing closer.

If it scented me
would it falter midfall
be somehow quirked alive,

its every sense
beside itself, revealed
as we would like to be –

the ecstasy
once given
going on and on.

III

A half-sense, a particular
grey light,
the way that wall of may

cascades across Holme Lane.
It's a circle
I can't break out of,

(niagara o roar
again), run it backwards,
forwards, whichever way,

there's that first moment
as night comes on –
the glim of falls

pallour of birch-limbs,
and that single note –
of water touching rock

touching air, touching
everything in reach,
and being changed by it

irrevocably,
from the very start –
knowing that much even then.

IV

Hiiiiii...
– was his calling card
the sound an easy falling

from delight
through resignation
into silence.

I hadn't thought
he'd reach this far
to the narrowing

upstream pools
maddened orange
by ferrous shales,

my eyes squinting
in the glare, as he
opens the door of the falls

and I stumble forward
close enough to know
the patterning

feeling it like a breath
on mine,
the exact sense of his skin.

V

White phosphorous.
He was gone
and the whole thing

hanging in the air.
Thereafter, endless tracing
of a journey never made,

love with no time
to fall clear of itself.
The strangest fire –

whelmed under cataracts
drenched, pummelled
but still burning

as it tumbles through the pool,
reassembling all the properties
of memory. Impossible

to find that same fall twice
however hard we try.
There was a wetting haar

as I remember, walking clear
not looking back
at the undiminishable image.

VI

Gorsed with frost
a world white over,
the river steaming.

His year's epiphany –
those two streams
thought and sperm.

How he waded in
placed one thing on another –
strings of blue milk

curding on water
drawn smooth to the brink,
where poured pitch

flipped to silver
in the leap
the smashed grains glittering.

One gout
snagged in a side-pool, refused this,
tracked round and round

below a lint-white tree, then it too
eased through
and over.

VII

The mind on nothing –
an absence-seizure
staring in the pool,

pourings, double-twists
and spirals, the ear
of countless inner surfaces

quelled to circles
dwindling vortices
as the mind shelves under,

substance separate from matter –
a stone on the pool-bed
the weight of a boulder

that shudders upright,
trembling on the current
on a balance

of densities,
a heart
a bubble

slowly buoyed
to the surface
of a cold, clear night.

THE LAKE #2

That blue!
Isn't it just the best you've ever seen?
So good you want to cry sometimes
that the minutes must crowd by
and the sky cloud over,
drag you on from here,
to something less close to love.

You could wait weeks
for such a morning. No quiver on the lake,
no limit to the cloudlessness.
The colour of calm.
The colour of no disappointment.
If one plane can illuminate another,
surely love will throw light on love.

And the stillness of the hill,
undermined by its own reflection,
dangling head-first into the void.
Here's the salvage to annihilation,
a mirror on what comes after.
No one can hurt us but ourselves.
We are, for now, inviolate in blue.

III

HALFWAY THROUGH THE KISSING GATE

IN PERUGINO'S GARDEN

I

We might stretch up a hand from the lounger
to free a fig or a spill of almonds,
or let them, when we're good and ready, fall to us.

Lotus-hour. Only the cypress stays upright,
ticking off its shadow (so less sombre than itself)
for being flat on its back and loving it.

I love it here, you say. How we imagined this
and now enact it, thought by thought,
you couldn't squeeze a wish between the two,

the gap as slender as the Via Baciadonna,
narrowest of the city's hugging streets,
the width, so it is claimed, of a woman's kiss.

II

A late-flying butterfly, the bat
sank to the cup of a night-flowering lily, sipped.
Pipestrello. Bella di Notte.

With the lightest touch of your hand, you show me this.
What takes a lifetime to find
is the sweeter to taste.

III

A red cap in Italy, so Leigh Hunt said,
goes by you not like a mere cap, but like what it is
an intense example of the colour red.

So with olive trees – blue-grey, grey-blue, then paling echoes
down to almost-white. Or silver, when they wrestle wind.
Behind, a hill of sunflowers cindering to brown.

IV

The calm of the loggia. Each element
in due relation to the other. A three to two proportion
for the main façade, an eight-ribbed dome

above the perfect cube of the Choir.
Mathematics and aesthetics as two sides
of the same coin. Fugue as measurable space.

What you regretted most was having no time left
to climb the cupola, step out above the city
and be your own defining centre, non-linear.

Uccello, when his wife called him to bed, would keep on
painting (con brio) saying what a sweet thing perspective is.
To each his own, Paolo, to each his own.

THE UNDER GARDENER

All day she sets the thing to rights,
her shrubs, *her* lawns, exactly as she pleases.
Only the weather sways her,
and the ground she works with.

She takes a long time answering the phone.
I was by the drive, she says, *while the light held.*
Her touch when she turns to me
is what I can't get enough of.

Wisteria. Azalea. It's these I'm minded of.
But typically, it's something wild she remembers.
Spring in Calling Wood, for instance.
The trees still bare, but the floor

already canopied in leaf. Bluebell.
Dog's mercury. A thousand
unwrapped mirrors glossing back at her.
She stares and stares.

There was *something that day,* she says,
what silence hints at,
the breath of the invisible.
How could we hope to match such things?

Come to bed, I tell her, *make love.*
But her eyes have that quiet and a light in them
that I can't get enough of
when she turns to me.

THE GROUNDS IN FEBRUARY

Early Flowering Rhododendron

I stood there, once more the dutiful lover.
She showed up, not dead at all but burning off dead ground,
trailing a log in flames behind her, a log
carved with the letters of the word: *Imagine.*

Gorse

You remember how, in that sailing heat
in that thrifted summer, you took her
flush to your face, breathed in deep
until you found (you thought) her heart.

Giant Hogweed

At what point is it we suddenly realise
the world won't get any taller or wider,
and the things acquired years ago, with no thought
beyond the short term, will be ours now till we die.

Hazel Catkins

We have broken after all these years
our gorgeous secrets, all our crazes
there at the world's mercy. Touch them gently
in case you harm yourself for life.

Snowdrops

Maybe it's delusion, maybe nothing of this matters
to a soul, but as I set the last poem aside, went to the shelves
and found Werther's *Sorrows* and Milosz's *Winter Bells*,
such a happiness urged forward, wanting nothing in reply.

Snowdrop

She tells me that in French it's *snow-pierce*,
and I can't get over how she stared that extra second
(her in her dark blue coat, me in my dark blue sweater)
the first moment we shook hands. Nor how this too,
        must vanish.

THE OBSESSION

It's like leaving a note for Diane who cleans here –
a sheet of A4 burdened with semen and her name,
then screwed up, tossed in the bin. So you're sure
if she thinks of you at all, she'll be fingering
the worksheets thrown away, unrolling that twist of paper.

*

Or later, waking from sleep with her voice still there
inside your head, you grab another sheet and fill it
instantly, without a second thought,
illumining the page in the name of a stranger,
hour after hour after hour.

*

Afterwards you switch off the anglepoise, sink back
and hear the tap tap tap of the newly screwed up sheet
opening out of its own volition in the waste bin,
as though it meant to, really meant to come alive
this time. That's what this whole thing's like.

KNOWLEDGE

Because fire was a property of trees
or flint, for those who first discovered it,
to a kid like me, of eight or so, fields
were all I ever knew of sex.

Summer. The grass chest-high. You could crawl
halfway through or more, as near them as you dare,
knowing you mustn't get too close, in case
they chased and murdered you. But you could listen.

That's why in the barn, I just had to.
Bales stacked to the rafters, we were pressing down
on a dozen sweltered meadows.

The world might break in at any moment.
I held your face in my hands.
Someone nearby was splitting logs.

VICTIM

No dream. No fantasy. Last night a woman dropped from the
sky
into my living room. She crashed through the window, strapped
to an airline seat.
I got up, there she was. From the back especially, she reminded
me of someone.

The crash investigators kept sealing the room. I kept breaking in.
I worked out between us, we had five kids, had been married
three times
(unfaithfully no doubt), and had now lost everything except
this house.

I could say to her – and did – *I feel terrible tonight, feel like*
shooting myself. And she wouldn't say – 'oh' – the way you register
the rain's begun, or the bin men have been. There was
crumble for tea.

I wasn't going to bother, but there it is – someone drops in
and you make the effort. You get to thinking this might be the
start of something,
and before you know it – you think it is.

Then a van pulls up, and the no-nonsense knocking grows more
and more
impatient. She wore the kind of clothes I liked. Her legs were
open slightly.
She would, I'm sure, have done me the same service, had the
roles been reversed.

HALFWAY THROUGH THE KISSING GATE

NO MAN'S LAND

When he stepped across the room to kiss her,
she pushed him away, saying *Shoo, shoo.*

Why she did this after so many hints
and come-ons, was she was scared stiff, she said.

Perhaps being wanted is enough, she added.
Something he had never considered.

Next day, a letter – three short lines about the squall
passing over, light returning, the lake

collecting up what was left of itself. No signature . . .
What note? she said, when he phoned her later.

I sent no note. What on earth would I say?
About what? To whom? Tell me that.

CLEARWAY

She happened (a bit suspiciously, he thought)
to be driving past as he walked home. *Happy Birthday!*

came the voice through the sunroof, *Want a lift?*
Once inside however, he felt like a gasman she was dealing with –

clipped sentences, eyes turned away. What Vicki said
came back to him – how Brad's idea of foreplay

was to plonk his willie on her lap while making coffee,
which nine times out of ten they didn't drink.

This translates instantly to Shoo Shoo's kitchen,
her laying down the cheeseboard to give her hand a wash.

Let's meet sometime, he offers, getting out.
I'm blocking traffic, she says, reaching for the door.

A OR B?

He tries again: – If, when I next come round,
you open the door and place your fingers to your mouth

and then to mine, lead me upstairs (the single goldfish
gulping hard), no greeting, no gossip

no excuses or postponements, I won't
I promise, say a single word. Or if

instead, you say: *Hallo. Come in. Some cheese?*
Some wine? How's the garden coming on?

We'll chat and drink, won't say another word
about it. – *But it's not A or B,* she answers.

Can't it be somewhere in between? – Tell me, he asks,
Your other goldfish, does he have a name?

EXHIBITIONISTS

Saw you in town the other day, she said,
you looked high and mighty and not that handsome.

It's Guppy's turn to sham indifference. He's sitting at her
kitchen table.
Has she, he wonders, stood outside in the field at night

watching him strip in the low light of the anglepoise?
Improbable, but nothing would surprise him.

I'd love to see you get undressed, he says, Just that, that's all.
I'd have to slim down first, she answers, but throws out her chest

as she does so, stands closer, pulling back
the two wings of her blouse a little, which is what

enflamed him in the first place. They're within an inch
of his face – that close, when he settles back. Looks away.

WHITE

Thanks for calling round, she said, *I'd still be in bed*
otherwise. No reason to get out.

She had his favourite jumper on, the white one
that showed things to advantage. Naturally

on leaving, he tempts her to the pantry for a private
parting hug. *No way*, she says. But straight after,

steps forward with: *I do love you you know,*
and a peck on the lips. Which he elaborates,

mauling her front as he does so.
Outside, the swifts are back, the last pink

burns from the blossom. He's astonished.
All she says is, *I'm glad your hands are clean.*

IV

SCENES FROM THE CUTTING-ROOM FLOOR

FLASHBACK (MAY, LIKE A DREAM)

It was still there, beached between trees,
a dew-webbed coracle of grass, the nap
laid flat in all directions, like two seas
their currents meeting cross-twined off some cape,
discarded tissues where two shapes had been.

When Liz appears she's in a white frilled blouse
and flared green skirt (the better to love her in),
the woodbed charmed upright from its wicker sleep.
Oh, it was Dave once, flattening the stems,
liloed on the rocking shadows of the leaves,
Liz, straddled over him, a mottled up-view
of leaf-dazzled breasts and stars of sunlight,
close up of a half closed eye, or underbreast –
skin tented outwards by a frantic heart.

They walk off quietly, to bathe in heat.
Dave stares, wishing he was there with her.
Passion and an unsalved lust, he wants it all
played over, see it this time from above,
to scrutinise their love – his comic bum,
its last gasp effort, her leg-play jigging
them over for a photo-finish. Nothing lost,
the coverage for once intact, complete.

He settles for an underview of trees.
A chestnut dips, its flared white candles
doyled round with green. Deep undulations.
A leaf husk dwindles down. Far off,
splashings of sunlight on the legs of lovers
entering at the shallows of the wood.

LIKE A CAST LINE, THE BUZZ OF THE STRIP LIGHT

Flicker and glare, the chuckling flow of gossip
purling from the general office. Almost lunchtime
when Liz phoned, canteen smells wafted up
through windows – fish again. She sounded different:

Dave, are you alone? Ray clattered set squares
on the other board. *I'm not,* he said, *I'll come straight*
down to you. (Pausing by the Gents of course,
his hair a mess, but it would do.) She was
in the corridor waiting. At the corner
they almost bumped. He could smell her breath – anxious, close:

I hope, she said, *you didn't think I was*
ignoring you. That was it, he had her.
Finally the bait was taken.
Likewise that moment, she had reeled him in.

BLACKBERRYING

They were dying for release, to give themselves
away – fattest, sweetest berries first
at the stalk's tip, at the slightest probe
of our blushed fingers. So many, so ripe,
that after each stripped bush, our scored hands
quickened to the next. An illicit bloom
wound over and around us. He watched my breasts
their sway and reach within the billowed blouse.

This gathering, *he said*, disturbs the dead
of ages – all those who surfaced here knew this by heart.

His wife, my husband – a town away.
Only the company of birds confined us.
Under a darkened looming sky we stood,
waiting the first tumbling touch.

INAUGURATIONS

You can find anything under hedgerows –
old clothes, trash, a bedstead overwintering
in haws, the wet rag of a magazine,
some boy of twelve, hair-trigger prick in hand,
teasing back the stuck layers of a centrefold.

Looking back, it's hard to believe – her feet
braced on the dashboard, my entering so
slick. Oh she was beautiful; I, outmatched,
couldn't make it, would have tried for hours
but the mist was clearing, another car
came lumbering through the dips.
How I raced
the two miles home, came flushed and late. All evening
raised full spread the image of those legs,
while the book I fingered got itself read.

PARTY

Had she stopped her ears with small talk, stayed deafened
in the downstairs rooms, or locked herself
in arguments on women's rights (helping
with the vol au vents), she would have been OK,
but the music's wild aortic beat drew her
upstairs, across the landing, through the door
to where Dave sat, turning the hi-fi louder
as she stepped inside, then louder still
to blind his words, arching himself towards
her beckoned ear, and in one motion
hands on waist, quick-centred her like clay.

Now Liz can't think or sleep or feel without
his arms on her, and he has turned the music
down, is brushing something off his jeans.

BURSTING THE CLOUDS (THE CHINESE CALLED IT)

How apt, that when we make love in the car
I kneel in front of you, and your body
comes towards me, as towards a supplicant.
Cunt-first. Truly, our heaven exists. In twenty
or thirty places that will never again
be of this world. To make the whole world other
than itself, should be our one devotion.
From this point on, working ever outwards:
Late night offices. A moonlit mountain.
Trains. A curtained cubicle. A bench somewhere.
Warm seas. Some Antipodean layby
as dark and close as this one.
These for starters,
thoughts to add to. As a sudden sweep of headlights
lofts us into brightness, like a sunlit arm.

MOMENTO AMORI

Letters, a polaroid remembrance in the drawer.
Void, vacuity, unstaunchable loss.
Today his absence has such presence,
stronger now than when I hold him. Nothing helps.

Those hours together. Their after-image
overprints on everything. I see him there
beside me in the full-length mirror, standing naked,
his brow against the shadow of my chin.

The first attempts were shaky, badly lit,
two bleached white figures concealing themselves
one against the other, from the dark inquisitor
of the lens. I, smiling, to see him turn in profile
at the last, bury his lips, nose, eyes
into my hair. Then we perfected it.

FROM THE BOOK OF A HUNDRED FACTS

I

The body goes straight to you, comes straight to me.
In perfect silence, with a lick of flame,
the air balloon, all silver, dreams itself alive
from a valley one mile distant – slow, for the sky
is viscous, skeined with evening, and the mare in foal
stands belly deep in buttercups, at ease.

From the meadow, an arm lifts clear of the skim
of moonpennies, into bronze light, as if to ring
that wisp of cirrus curling from the east.

Time moves slow across the skin. A second shadow
lengthens, another hand brushing light
on that lifted arm, till fingers clasp and bind.

In perfect silence, with a lick of flame,
The body goes straight to you, comes straight to me.

II

You were on your back, eyes closed, arms out, your clothes
beside you. There was the sound of a plane
in the distance, voices from across the lake.

It was the time when water crowfoot slows
the current – daisy beds buoyed high into the light,
so the young coot in grey velvet can snow-step
bank to bank, while a bullock meanders
through an uncut field that could keep him sweet
through the longest winter.

In the grass – fragments
of speckled shell, a downy scattering of feathers
broadcast through the stitchwort, the white and red
campion. I might have pulled you from the river
you lay so still, were you not so warm
to my finger, or smiling quite so much.

HOME TRUTHS AT MIDNIGHT

Again! They come together. *You on me*
this time. She quickens. Bone to bone. The suck
and slough of flesh. *Hard. Harder.* Then release.
All definition melts. Then the thought
that he must leave, and therefore lose her.

She senses it, watching him fumble into clothes,
forgo her warm sheets for the night outside,
drive home, touch eighty on the hill, swoop down
into the dead streets of another town,
another bed, another body, closed in sleep,
or a silence that resembles sleep, and lies
in silence, the church clock quartering the hours.

Back there, she's up, to lock the door, turn out
the lights, is sitting naked on the stair.

BESTIARY

Wide Cheshire grins, when the bed began creaking
on the floor above. We listened in as creak
got louder and creaks got faster. Pictured her,
a vamp in snake-sheen, writhing on a frenzy
that with one prodigious creak fell silent.

Pictured him, a pig on two legs, reared up
on the sheets, a King Kong of pork, knuckles
to the ceiling beam, chest thrust out, breathless
phallus ticking its way down from 2 oclock
to 5, clearing its throat of one last glob
as it tracks past 3 in its declination.

Well we just laughed, up on all fours, one dog
to another, began our own perambulations.
Twelve midnight – one handed, straight up, twinned.

LUNCH ON THE GRASS

Woods, a lakeside. Leaf-lace and leopard mark
of sunlight. We sit, you still milk-naked,
I reclothed. Our picnic, the blue spread
of your dress discloses all. Not the first time
we've been caught. As though for real, your husband's
sitting close; while in the middle ground my wife
in earshot, studies grass, for what it lacks –
sweet hemp of sex.
                                        What else could match the day
as solidly, yet have no substance
so our hands go through on nothing, on a play
of light, dust-flecked and luminous,
where every break and hidden edge lines clear.
Your moment's face, outshown so flawlessly,
I see it hours from now, a sorry grey.

RUMBLED

Our lovers – scarfed in each other's arms, slow
intoxicated progress, each supporting each
along the road. At intervals, a mouth
resuscitates a mouth. Through blousey, violet
cumulus, the view into a tulip's throat –
sunset over sinful Sheringham on Sea.

At *The Imperial*, the *Helikon Hotspots*
are thumping it out in the foyer,
rip-roaring, sweaty bonhomie hits them
as they tumble through the doors, too absorbed
to notice the big surprise in the corner
who's just clapped eyes on them, and strewth!
is walking over with a smirk this wide, blurts out
a real show-stopper of a *how-dy-do!*

SUNDAY, HIS VOID PERSONIFIED

Gale or no gale, out Pru stormed at 3 a.m.
Roof slates flew after her, chimney bricks
swept full-lock overhead, met glass somewhere,
some swinging gate knocked hell out of its frame.

Next morning, out of hours, by Hebden's shop,
a glazier, arms outstretched, miming himself,
hoisting something wide from van to waiting frame.

Imagine, how he ran a finger down the sheet's
cold spine, brought it to an edge, then split it clean.
Now see, he wipes his handiwork away,
to leave the drab street mirrored on itself,
or view what's left of yesterday's display –
a consort of shop mannequins, caught in
flagrante delicto, huffish, disarrayed.

MARTINS

Beginnings of loss, first fallen swarf of leaves,
finery and all elation gone. Outside
the keening of a robin's blade.
Dulled beat of neighbour hammering on walls.

For god's sake, take a hold of yourself!
Repeated twice, the voice she hates.
Dave hears, appalled, what issues from his mouth.

A grey barred sky, a fouled and hedged-in ground –
how different the white walled place that shimmered
at the starting out . . . A few days hunched in rain
and they were gone. Whether singly or in flocks,
the how of it remains unsolved. One morning
they were simply gone – sky blank, the under-eaves
in fragments, all the wires stripped bare.

LOVE LYING IN STATE, CHRISTMAS

Marriage now becomes marriage by numbers.

Pronounce it dead. A month of mouth-to-mouth
would not revive it now. The mistletoe,
the paper hearts bought love-struck moons ago,
lace out the rooms accusingly. We're neuter.
Can't or won't respond. Spent. At 38!
Our ten-year home as cosy as a morgue,
as sickening as turkey on the fourth day.

Shall I compare her to a winter's day –
grey from end to end. No warmth, no passion.
Dull. And this the best of it. At other times
count ten slowly, face away. Were I to look
there would be nothing there to please me.

Our love gone by on the arms of others.

CINÉMA VÉRITÉ

You bastard, bastard, bastard – suddenly
he's out, it's dark, he's running, the camera
hard on his heels, down the drive, to a car,
close-up as he gets inside, looks back for one
last time towards the house, starts the engine,
pulls away. The last shot – his face, in headlights,
in the rear-view mirror, a stranger's face
crying, saying it over and over.

Wide angle on the room – Liz hasn't moved, face
expressionless, indifferent, a stranger's face.
Flashback to that scene three months before –
her tears, sound outside, of a car leaving,
for the nth time, she's alone saying it
over and over – *You bastard, bastard, bastard.*

PENIS TALK

Compared with you, all the handwork in the world
won't do it. I've tried all ways to shuck away
the lust, the loss. No joy.
Think of the time
(twice at least) when the thing slipped off
on the second round, so I withdrew
when it came to it (sheened with sweat)
to find myself sheathed only in a film of you.
You fished around inside for ages,
while I withered.
But think too of your hand
clamped across it, as, wholly gutted
of every horny bone in our bodies,
you slid into trusting sleep, while I
eased you off, turned aside to sleep myself,
when I knew instead I should have held you.

MADONNA WAS NUMBER ONE AT THE TIME

They met, he and Liz, by what seemed like chance,
in the queue for lunch, on the seventh floor cafeteria.
So she was seeing someone else. *I guessed,*
he said, *last night, in a dream, it came to me.*
Of course, I'm happy for you . . . both.
(The last word took some forcing out.)

How strange, she said, *trust you to know my thoughts,*
coming closer, adding with that touch of hers,
But then we were always . . . close. (That word
would take some swallowing.) He plumped for chilli
and meringue; she, ham salad minus ham.

By what seemed like chance, the only two seats left
were face about, on separate tables.
Madonna was number one at the time.

DOUBLE VISION

She'd been away all day. He played a hunch
and headed for the woods – a love-car snuggled
under trees, wet light of murky afternoon.

He angled past pretending not to look
then doubled back inside the wood through whips
of underbrush, to find (the shock of it!)
someone his size already snooked up there,
a leaf-framed eye to the misting screen. Then
(shock on shock) to see that double turn around,
come stalking back for a better angle.

He froze. A blackbird cabled overhead.
From the leatherette, a face and the face
it mirrored, peeped out, peeped out . . .
Give me time, I will explain everything.

ROUGH TRADE

'Take this love-stone – it's my hand when I'm not there.'
I said that, I actually said that,
and mouthed 'I love you' how many times
before I, as she puts it: 'rushed away'.

Turns out that day, she meets this divorcee
in a restaurant. They were screwing within the hour.
'Protecting myself' is what she calls it,
'Not putting all my eggs . . .' etc.

I wanted to cry – couldn't. Wanted her to –
she didn't. Till I held her. Then what was broken
all poured out. And she was sorry, oh so
sorry. Doing it, she said, made her feel sick:
'All the time, my only thought was you.' I fucked her
how she wanted it – hard, with venom.

COMING DOWN WITH IT

How you dilate, and dripping, flow for me.
I browse small wings of flesh – a pink skinned bird
whose pinion craves the air and my cool tongue.

Do it like a dog, you say, and watch us
in the mirror, our skins together
like veneers.
Everything is dangerous.
Eating is a risky business. They're taking down
the Show tents in a swift-hung dusk,
a farewell disco in the last marquee,
a barbecue, with people in a line –
some I know, so I keep on walking.

In five weeks you'll have flown away,
perhaps for ever. Tonight's a first rehearsal
for that day. I think about it all the time.

SWITCHBACK

I need time, she says (this justifies anything
she cares to name), *let's leave it for a while.*

Those August evenings he searched out her car
left notes, sweet peas beneath the wiper blades.
Last week she paid him back by *not* walking
the twenty yards it took to do the same.

He's a three-year-old that's close on forty.
He's sly and mixed up and must be punished.
She gives him time to write out all these lines.

He killed a lamb once, pressed its head into a pool
until the bubbles stopped. Astonishing, how long
a weak, crow-blinded thing can cling to life.

Have it your way Liz. It's finished! The look
she gave him – a fool might call it love.

HER COMING CLEAR

Witch doctor to a seven-week-long drought,
when I arrived, rain fell, then would not stop.
Jilted, but still on fire for him – two states
that won't lie down, one with the other. Got up
finally at dusk, to the sink, to retch
the whole thing out. That first remark he made
still gags: If no one knows, no one gets hurt.

Over Colonsay, late evening angles clear,
breaks east into this bay, sidelights a stage-flat
piece of shore and lifts it, an unworldly green,
to unexpected prominence. The sea seems
drugged, a seal-flop motion, as the week's last
ferry pirouettes away – someone on deck
waving a long time at the emptying pier.

HIS RUINED LARCH

How little's underneath it all. The line of larch
that plumed the hill, toppled in a bitter storm,
the star-grasp of their roots, cuffed round with earth,
snatched sideways to the sun; bare rock beneath
the torn-back turf, as close as knuckle-bone to flesh.

How little nourishment there was, or hold.
The branches tuft blood-red with flower spikes,
one last out-oozing of the fire, while living
trees smoke-thicken round a flush of green.
And now it rains, woods slicked and dripping.

Head down, I pour through lanes, regarding little,
and that deceit, or false hopes poorly pinned.
Her voice comes flat over the phone – always
finally alone, the line scored out, gone dead.

LIZ AND THE SALTIRE

I'm reading Updike and this line jumps out:
'The wrong guy had made a move on her,
she came east to get her head together.'
For east read north – it's as simple as that.

He can't see it, says he'll fight for love, demands
I do the same, says silence tortures him.
So I write. He yells back by return:
'Your letter's full of shit'. Thinks that will rod the bends
of our relationship. It's laughs I need, not this.

Oh look – a coot, picking through the river's crud.
Careful, it's a minefield here, it says NO DOGS
but who reads signs. See that sky-wide cross
of vapour trails – he'd read a 'kiss' where 'no' was meant,
see victory in the weals of defeat.

SCARS

I've these three horizontal scars, across
the small of my back. Nothing happened
that I or my mother can remember.
They were there at birth. Proof perhaps (who knows)
of some much older wounding. A past life
printed on the present. Which might explain,
compounding the improbabilities,
the mess we've made of things so far.
You and I wrecking a life together.
Then meeting up again and wrecking this.

The wounded fall towards their wounds. 5 a.m.,
the last star. Someone, as the day racks skyward,
walking somewhere from somewhere else,
seeing nothing. Having seen it all before.

WAKING THE CELLO

Dave drove west into the sun to see her
one last time, thinking of the dark drive back.
Instead, she held him all night. Like a dream,
waking to drive east into the sun.

Then, one week on, the car that brakes suddenly,
for no apparent reason. Till someone gets out
slams the door on someone left inside.

You're mean. Unsociable. You're badly dressed.
Don't ask Liz why she yells these things.
Or why, in a few days when he comes back,
she opens the door to him with a look
which says: – *OK you shit, just one more time.*

She held out her hand. He opened her robe.
They lost their resolution, reversibly.

DAVE AND THE CURRIED SOUP

The trouble with Jerusalem artichokes –
they make you fart too much afterwards.

I thought perhaps what pissed you off, was backsliding
on some resolve you'd made regarding us.
The interregnum altered nothing. Only the car
had changed, a new front seat to worry about, a sunroof
full of moon. Despite which, all the usual signs –
fucked up, can't sleep, your squirming of a finger
up my anus, by easy stages, getting hooked.

But so what. March is on its feet again. Untouched.
And the magnolia! I can't keep my eyes
clear of it, my fingers to myself. Come soon.

It tasted good by the way. I loved it.
Though a little more fenugreek I think – next time.

THE WILMSLOW MOVE

Ugh! It's sweaty! She let go the hand he offered,
strode ahead to the restaurant. The talk
over chicken fricasseé, was touchy, forced.
In the pub he slid an arm along her shoulder.

I feel positive tonight, she said. *This move was the best*
I ever made. Outside, unexpectedly,
she linked arms, even took his soppy palm
in hers. In the car she wanted MORE.

Why two hours, he asked, *to get this far? To prove*
you're in control? He turned first right on Dean Road
back to her new place. *Perhaps so,* she whispered.

No shock therefore with him lying naked,
and her still half undressed at the foot of the bed,
when she said, *I want you to go. Now!*

PIGS

They talked about themselves only in the imperfect.
They were there. They were happy. Once.
She said this always after sex. A gambit
meant to cut love dead. It did so every time.

This time she simply upped the stakes with: *It was never
really love.* And: *I can smell your fucking feet.*

Remembrance Day. Parades brassing up the hill.
Dave spades the lot into the soil. Oompahs,
bonfire ash and weeds, the robin's blade,
their last night, the sheer invulnerability
that will one day fix a sneer onto her face.
Should she weaken, he'll be ready with his own clean edge:

*When you're the same person two days running,
phone me. I'll be off flying with the pigs.*

LAST RITES

They'd been lifting 'skellies' from the ground all week,
bagging them for reinterment. Each day
I'd go along to watch. It was something to do,
though in your tems I was 'festering'.
By contrast, you were never home.

Barrowload on barrowload of debris
hit the skip. Gradually the new path took shape.

I read how Lord Lovel lost his bride
on their wedding night. They were playing
hide and seek, but the dead-lock on the oak chest
spring-snapped tight. No trace. Her father
went insane. Lovel threw himself into a war.

They found her skeleton years after.
Apocryphal no doubt – but it suited me.

It was all OK, till you unearthed the note
you'd spent the whole morning searching for.
It could have been to anyone. If it mentioned you
in less than glowing terms, you didn't want to know.

They found two intermingled, radius
and digits across the other's femur.
The sorting out was somewhat difficult.
They were stained clay-brown. And brittle,
a shard of skull like a piece of crispbread.

How long have you known you didn't want me?
Two months? Three? What brought it irreversibly

to light, was just now hearing you say:
'I thought I ought to mention – Bill's coming
this weekend.' I put the phone down. Stunned.

Before tea, they unearthed a lead coffin
by the West Door, still intact.
As they slewed it gently into deeper ground,
a seam burst, and liver-brown consommé
poured into the soil.

I spend an hour searching for the blue
eye-shadow you'd left among my things,
and now need back. No trace.
The books you gave me – Have them instead!
I bag them up. Tomorrow will be our last meeting.

Love-shit. Corpse-gruel. You can take so much
before your stomach turns.
Incredible, it took this long.
But tonight I sleep like a baby.

FADE-OUT (SIBYLLINE WORDS)

In the geri-ward at the Royal, Uncle Bill
drifts in from dinner wearing two ties
and his fly undone. *It's a madhouse here,*
he says. Then softly: *Your auntie and me*
we were like THAT. He gestures a fist
but it's love he means. A janitor,
half-packet of McVities in one hand,
strolls across to a corner table.
A nurse there, leans back with a cuppa.
They grin at each other. Dave looks away.

There's a woman banging on the table
with both hands – left, right, paddling away for hours.
The man beside her endlessly picking
at the curtains. Till the nurse says *STOP!*)